time heals...

time heals...

{finding self love after a heartbreak}

Sarah Bagheri

Published by Tablo

Table of Contents

"Were You Bluffing?"

when my eyes met yours across the room,
I felt my heart skip a beat.

we exchanged names, and the next thing I know,
we were standing on that silly little rotten dock, and

you said those three words.

you made me feel whole,
until your touch gradually became nothing.

was that your goal?
when you said you loved me were you bluffing?

"I Wish You Weren't Lying"

Gradually falling in love with everything about you,
the way your curly brown hair fell around your ears
and that crooked smile.
I told you that I was in love with you,
and you said it back,
but as your eyes wandered to a different place
and as your voice gave in.

At least one of us wasn't lying.

"daydream"

i was sitting at the shoreline,
watching the endless fields of blue,
go on and on,
forever.
which seems like how long i'll be waiting
for you.

"A Cigarette Type of Love"

I was the cigarette to your lighter,
with every touch you ignited a spark inside of me.
I saw the flame and as soon as it greeted me,
I felt every emotion that comes with love.
And with each hit you took,
I felt myself slowly becoming smaller and smaller.

I began to deteriorate.
My ashes became nothing more than worthless black
rubbish underneath your feet.
"Can't you feel me shrinking?"
"Don't you care" -
I whispered in a raspy tone.

With each inhale you took,
I was blindsided, thinking you wanted me,
But I was just your escape-

Until there was nothing left of myself.

"only if..."

as your words stumbled out of your mouth like honey
and your touch ignited thousands of butterflies,
love began to blossom inside of me.

only if you would have watered what you began to blossom,
maybe the love I had for you would not have faded away.
I still don't recall the exact moment

but gradually words stumbled out as the opposite of
honey
and the butterflies stopped visiting.
each day a new petal fell,

leaving me feeling hopeless.
only if you would have watered what you began to blossom.

"whirlpool"

you,
you make me feel like i am drowning,
yet, you're the only one who I find myself breathing by.
drowning in this toxic love,
swimming,
and swimming to the surface,
i finally get there, but now
i'm too exhausted,
so I sink back down

how do I get out of this whirlpool?

"But You Promised?"

And there we were, back at the dock with the rotten wood,
we stood there as tears streamed down both of our faces.

I was trying to let go,
but you promised me things would change.

I believed you as I looked into your promising blue eyes
and as you pulled me closer.

I decided we could try again,
We built our love back up again

only to watch it fall.
You promised me things would change,

Why did they never?

"Red Flags"

So many red flags
that I chose to ignore,
I thought they say that red stands for love.

The red flags tried to warn me.
But i'm finally slipping away on my own,
and now were just too broken to fix.

So please do not tell me you will turn your flags white,
because I am done giving you any more hope,
I've been let down one to many times by you,

and i'm tired.

"Now I'm More Than Alone"

your heart became my home,
i looked at you and saw our future.

now i'm more than alone,
giving up on you was the hardest decision i've had to
make.

loving you at your worst,
knowing you more than you do.

i tried so hard to lighten up your dark world.
you told me I was failing

you told me I was doing a horrible job
when I was giving you all I had and more.

its killing me slowly-

to know you need somebody to talk to
and that you may feel more alone than I do right now.

"When The Sun Goes Down"

watching the day turn into night
as the fresh air breezes through the car
and your voice fills up the car
as you sing to your favorite song -
for the few moments as you watch the sky change
colors,
you forget who you are
the few moments of pure bliss one desires to prolong

and then the sun goes down and the sky catches up to
my mood.

already, I wait for tomorrow,
when I get to forget again for a few moments

the brokenness.

"Trust Issues"

i whispered to you,
my insecurities-
and you sat there and scolded the men who gave them to
me.
you comforted me and rolled your eyes in disgust,
how did you cover it up so well?
      that you were one of them too.

"The Movie That Makes You Cry"

Moving on is hard when
you still consume all of my thoughts,
but our movie isn't screening anymore.
And it's hard to not rewatch your favorite movie.
We were characters that life decided to give new roles
too.
I just can't quite learn how to play this new role-
so until then, I will watch our movie instead
and maybe eventually it will hurt a little less.
And I will learn how to not dwell
on you not being the other main character.

"a soft spot"

the truth that hurts the most is
i'd let you do it again
because for some reason
i will forever have a soft spot for you

"As I Watch the Tears Stream Down my Face"

I wonder when I will finally be the girl everybody thinks
I am.
The high-spirited girl that smiles too much

I miss her.

I stand in front of my bathroom mirror trying
to not let my head to rerun what we once were
I give in, and now I'm
playing back our movie as I watch the tears stream down
my face

I wish we were one of those movies with a happy
ending.
Instead, we were the screening of one of those movies
that you leave the theatre still in tears.

I stand in front of my bathroom mirror as I allow my
head to rerun what we once were
playing back our movie as I watch the tears stream down
my face.

"that constant feeling"

people ask "how are you?"
and my mind thinks one thing, while saying another
if i told you, you would ask me why
and I don't even know the answer.
the constant feeling of _____.

the word I can't seem to ever describe
i have no reason to be not okay, and yet
i am far from okay
but I can't tell anybody because they will ask me "why"
and I do not know
why I always feel like _____.

"drowning in thoughts"

the sun went down
and through the open window,
i hear the rain fall through the trees.
the darkness is almost suffocating
but then some of the orange light finds it way
and creeps into my room.
drowning in thoughts,
i hate being alone.

"Can't Stop Dreaming of You"

I cant seem to get out of bed lately.
My alarm clock blares in my ear,
doesn't it know that I want to sleep for ten more
minutes,
who wouldn't when they're dreaming about you?
You are in all of my dreams,

and that is why I sleep so much.

"The Abandoned House"

We built up a home, from scratch.
And as we created stories in each room,
they were all painted with sticky paint.
We poured concrete on the floors and as it dried,
I found myself not being able to dance around the
kitchen with you anymore.
I felt stuck. Not being able to move.
I asked you if this house was a bad idea,
You told me it wasn't, and so we built it,
despite the lack of materials we had.
You said we could make it work.
You told me you loved me,
and as I told you my insecurities you told me to stop.
Stop overthinking,
But then you proved them true.
How could you bring somebody else into our home?
And the second I heard you tell me "I cheated",
our roof came in.
And I had to get out of this abandoned house.

"Homesick"

I lay in my bed, late at night
while the thunder crashes down and the only light,
is the sporadic lightning that strikes down.

I'm cuddled up in your sweatpants,
listening to our favorite songs.
And it was then I realized,
you can be homesick for people too.

"Tears Playlist"

It's not that I liked to be sad
but it's all I had felt for so long,
that I learned to grow comfortable
with my burdening emotions.
And then you came along-
and it was then that I realized
I only pushed you away because
I found comfort in my sadness.
I guess all I can do now is shuffle my tears playlist,
like I always do.
Maybe the next time we meet, I would have taught
myself
how to get out

and there can be more to us.

"that sweet and sticky syrup"

you softly say those four words,
"but i love you"
and you flood my phone with
apologies -

 i mistake your words as sweet syrup.
the thing i always seem to want,
yet forget the sticky mess
that i always end up having to clean up-

alone.

"love the little things"

challenge yourself to fall in love with the little things-
sunshine beams down on my hand as wind tangles up
my hair
and a smile reaches across my face,
the feeling one wished would stay.
challenge yourself to let go of the things that may not be
fair

fall in love with your morning cup of coffee
as the steam rises
from your favorite mug with the silence of the morning.
and learn to admire the finish of the orange mug,
glossy.
think about the small things, and
they suddenly become charming

"Water Yourself"

There was a time when I passed a mirror,
and for the first time when I saw my reflection staring
back at me,
I was not a stem. I was greeted by my reflection with
colorful petals waving back at me.
Life got better when I learned that I have to water
myself.
When I learned how to do things that lead to growth,
when I tried new things,
I saw myself starting to blossom.
Self-love grows with patience.
and effort.
When I feel my petals drying up, I look for the sun.
And begin to water myself.
I reach for the paintbrushes in the back of my desk,
I go for a walk,
I look for the good.
So that when I pass a mirror again, I see colorful petals
waving back at me.
Sometimes a petal may fall, and
I do feel helpless, but I just remind myself that,
Life got better when I learned that I have to water
myself.

"Rock Bottom"

I loathed in my rock bottom for a while,
longer than needed,
allowing the rocks to bruise and skid across my skin.
And then I got up, and as I started climbing up the
staircase
towards self-love,
the bruises healed and the skid marks faded.
Although I still have scars, they are healed,
and are now just reminders of how far I've come.

"A Poem Romanticizing the Moon"

People tend to ask me why I love the night time,
and why the dark sky brings me peace.
The glowing light of the moon shines down,
illuminating the water and making the owls sing.
The neighboring stars welcome the moon,
with disregard to the shape the moon holds that night.
A waning crescent
A full moon
Gradually changing, into distinct phases,
each of which holds their own charm.
Always shining its light,
I fell in love with the moon
because it is a reminder, change is growth.
Whatever phase we may be in,
however dark our surroundings,
we can still radiate light.
The moon teaches us that no matter how small we feel,
we can still glow,
So our neighbors will always welcome us too,
As the stars do to the moon.
And that is why I am in love with the night time.
Because of the moon.

"Tend to Your Own Garden"

A lesson that was hard to learn:

You can't wait for somebody to bring you a vase
filled with beautiful flowers-
Instead just plant the seeds yourself
And learn how to grow your own garden,

it is the best thing you can do for yourself.

"first love"

when your asked about your first love
how wonderful it would be if you said "myself"
what a beautiful thought it would be
to be so proud of your soul

"Blurring Out the Past"

It's not that you need to forget
everything that happened-
and blur it all out. not think about it-
cause then what if we repeat history.
And that took me a while to learn-
how to be able to remember my past
without the tears,
and how to simply grow from it.
our past shapes us,
don't try and blur it out,
I promise eventually the hurt will fade away.

"the voice inside my head..."

oh, how I love the feeling,
the feeling of being content.
the voice in my head begs for it to stay,
as I rub my eyes.

oh, how I love the feeling,
the feeling of being content.
one day I noticed the voice in my head,
has found company elsewhere.

oh, how I love the feeling,
the feeling of being content.

and I love it more when the feeling stays.

the voice that once begged this feeling to stay,
is now a companion with feeling of content.
and as the voice grew to accompany this feeling-
it learned what makes it blossom,
what makes it fade away,
and how to stay by its side.

so now, when something is in my way-
the voice in my head now begs me to act differently.
and it feels good-
to finally be at a place where the voice in my head

is a friend to me too.

"Time Heals"

your hand softly touches mine
and for the first time,
since him

I felt those butterflies again.
the pain does fade away,
listen to them when they tell you that -

time heals.